## DATE DUE

|  |  |  |  |
|---|---|---|---|
|  |  |  |  |
|  |  |  |  |
|  |  |  |  |
|  |  |  |  |
|  |  |  |  |
|  |  |  |  |
|  |  |  |  |
|  |  |  |  |
|  |  |  |  |
|  |  |  |  |
|  |  |  |  |
|  |  |  |  |
|  |  |  |  |
|  |  |  |  |
|  |  |  |  |
|  |  |  |  |
|  |  |  |  |
|  |  |  | PRINTED IN U.S.A. |

DIGITAL AND INFORMATION LITERACY ™

# BIG DATA AND YOU

MINDY MOZER

rosen publishing's
**rosen central**®

New York

Published in 2015 by The Rosen Publishing Group, Inc.
29 East 21st Street, New York, NY 10010

Copyright © 2015 by The Rosen Publishing Group, Inc.

First Edition

## Library of Congress Cataloging-in-Publication Data

Mozer, Mindy, author.
Big data and you/Mindy Mozer. — First edition.
    pages cm. — (Digital and information literacy)
Audience: Grade 5–8.
Includes bibliographical references and index.
ISBN 978-1-4777-7643-8 (library bound)—ISBN 978-1-4777-7645-2 (pbk.)—
ISBN 978-1-4777-7646-9 (6-pack)
1. Big data–Juvenile literature. 2. Electronic data processing—Juvenile literature.
3. Business—Data processing—Juvenile literature. 4. Information technology–Juvenile literature. I. Title. II. Series: Digital and information literacy.
QA76.23.M69 2014
004—dc23

2014000795

*Manufactured in the United States of America*

# CONTENTS

# INTRODUCTION

A student searches for information for a research paper using Google. Another student sends a text to a friend. A third student buys groceries at the local supermarket and swipes a store shopper's card to take advantage of some discounts.

Each time you use a computer or a cell phone or log on to a social media site like Facebook or Twitter, you create data. Think about how many times you, your friends, your classmates, and your family use computers and other digital devices, and how often. Now think about how many people in the United States, Canada, and the rest of the world do the same thing. That is a lot of data being created—data that includes a lot of valuable information about you and everyone else who uses information technology.

The collection of that kind of data, the organization of it, and the analysis of it is called "Big Data."

Big Data has taken on new importance because computers only recently have had the power to process such mindboggling amounts of data and because companies, governments, and other organizations can afford the technology to store and study the data.

Companies use Big Data to come up with new products such as television shows and video games. Some companies use Big Data to figure out what products to stock on store shelves and to predict what their customers

When a person uses a cell phone, she creates data. Big Data is the collection of all this data, the organization of it, and the analysis of it.

will want to buy in the future. Internet companies such as Amazon.com use Big Data to suggest products to customers with the hope of increasing sales.

Governments use Big Data to improve bus transportation, the flow of traffic, parking, and even to reduce the rat population. Police departments use Big Data to catch criminals. Health care organizations use Big Data to monitor flu outbreaks, develop new drugs, and better treat patients.

Advocates of Big Data say the benefits include improved health care and government services, as well as personalized shopping experiences that will save buyers time and money.

But not everyone sees Big Data as a good thing. Some people worry about their privacy. Should companies and governments have access to what people search for on the Internet or write in text messages? Should companies track purchases made at their stores? Should police departments be able to create profiles of criminals and then stop people who match those profiles, even if they may not have done anything illegal?

Big Data is complicated and gets more complicated as businesses and organizations use it to uncover patterns and trends. Time will tell the real value of Big Data.

# Chapter 1

# What Is Big Data?

To understand Big Data, let's start by explaining data. Data is factual information organized in a way that can be analyzed. Big Data is exactly what it sounds like—a massive amount of data that is so big, it can't be processed using traditional methods.

Big Data can consist of billions to trillions of records. It is sometimes classified as petabytes or exabytes. How big is a petabyte? All research academic libraries take up two petabytes. How big is an exabyte? It would include all words ever spoken by human beings.

Every minute, people create data using their computers, cell phones, and Global Positioning System (GPS) devices. Data comes from sensors, which send signals about how things, such as trains and airplanes, are working. Data comes from comments and photos posted on social media, such as Facebook and Twitter.

Some of this data is unstructured, which means that it can't be stored in an easy-to-read manner, such as rows and columns. But when this information becomes structured and when different sets of data are cross-referenced or looked at together, it can provide clues to future trends in everything from

People create data with their computers, cell phones, GPS devices, and tablets every minute. That's a lot of data being created.

business to sports to science to medicine. The challenge is figuring out a way to organize the data to find patterns, and how to make those patterns meaningful.

## Big Data Is Not New Data

Although the term "Big Data" has caught on recently as technology has improved and become cheaper for companies, people have been using data to predict behavior for a long time.

In 1956, IBM announced the 305 and 650 Random Access Memory Accounting data-processing machines, which used disks for storage. IBM described the products as stacks of disks that stored millions of facts and figures. The company said at the time that the machines "show business as it is right now, not as it was hours or weeks ago."

Baseball fans have also been manipulating facts and figures to predict outcomes for decades. In the mid-1970s, Bill James began studying baseball box scores to try to figure out why teams win and why they lose.

For example, in baseball, a player's performance is often reflected in his batting average, which is figured out by dividing the number of hits by the number of times the player is at bat. But James realized there is more to a player than a batting average. Two players might have the same batting average, but one of those players might hit more home runs than the other player. The player who hits the home runs would be more valuable to the team because his hits score runs, and runs win games.

James called his method sabermetrics. SABR comes from the Society of American Baseball Research. James wrote books about sabermetrics, but his ideas didn't get a lot of attention until a book called *Moneyball: The Art of Winning an Unfair Game* was published in 2003.

*Moneyball: The Art of Winning an Unfair Game* was about Billy Beane, who used data in a similar way in the 1990s. Beane played baseball in the 1980s in the minor leagues and then six seasons in the major leagues. In 1990, he became a part of the management team of the Oakland Athletics, and in 1997, he was named general manager. Rather

General manager Billy Beane of the Oakland Athletics stands in the clubhouse during a spring training workout in February 2012 in Phoenix, Arizona. He used data to make decisions about his baseball team.

than basing decisions on how successful a player was in the last game played, he started using statistics to make decisions for the team, such as which players to trade and who should be in the lineup. His goal was to field the best team he could without spending a lot of money on players. A movie called *Moneyball* based on the book came out in 2011, starring Brad Pitt as Billy Beane.

In recent years, technology has improved and there has been an explosion of data in many fields. Social media sites, such as Facebook, are constantly collecting data—2.5 billion pieces of content a day and more than 500 terabytes of data a day. This data has created more opportunities for researchers.

# Big Data Today

Collecting data is the first piece of Big Data. To understand how Big Data is used today, think about a typical trip to the grocery store and a grocery store receipt. The receipt shows the date and time the purchase was made, the items that were purchased, and how the items were paid for. In addition, if the customer swiped a loyalty or shopper's card from the store, the store has the customer's name, address, telephone number, a history of all purchases made by that customer, a history of the customer's coupon use, a history of the date and time of all purchases, and a history of how all past purchases were paid for.

The intriguing thing for the grocery store is to figure out what to do with all of this data. Some grocery store chains use the data to target customers and sell more products. For example, let's say a store wants to try to sell a new type of bread on the market. The most likely customers for that bread are people who buy similar brands. The store can use its database from its loyalty card program to create a list of all people who buy similar brands. Then the store can send those people coupons for the new brand in the mail

A grocery store receipt shows more than the products purchased at the store. The receipt can be full of data, especially if the customer swiped a shopper's card from the store.

or by e-mail. Customers who previously knew nothing about the bread are now introduced to the product.

The store can also use the data to predict future food trends. Perhaps a new item is selling well after it is introduced in one part of the country. Researchers could use this information when determining how much to order in other parts of the country.

Here are some other ways the data can be used:

- The store could track how items sell based on where they are located in a store. For example, do items sell better if they are placed up front by the cash registers?
- The store can track what day of the week people shop the most and the type of items they buy. Then grocery stores could change displays daily based on that data to appeal to what customers are buying.
- Stores can predict what will be a big seller in the future based on past selling trends.
- Stores can predict how weather will affect what people buy. Many years of data might show that the threat of a snowstorm, for example, makes people want to buy milk.
- The store could track how far people travel to shop and on what day of the week.

The Big Data at a grocery store in many ways has some structure and can be organized. The challenge with a lot of Big Data is that it isn't as easily organized.

Think about how often people use the Internet in a day. They might "like" something on Facebook. They might search a topic on Google for a research paper they have due. They might look up a word on Dictionary. com. Each time people do one of these things, a tiny bit of data is stored. That data alone is meaningless, but when it's put together with other data, researchers can use it to predict some things about the person who accessed the information.

File    Edit    View    Favorites    Tools    Help

ANSWER: WHAT IS WATSON?

# Answer: What Is Watson?

In 2011, a computer system competed on the popular game show *Jeopardy!* against former winners Brad Rutter and Ken Jennings. The computer system was developed by IBM researchers and named Watson after Thomas J. Watson, the founder of IBM.

Watson is a supercomputer that can make sense of Big Data quickly. It had access to two hundred million pages of stored content it could search to answer questions during the game show. Watson beat both Rutter and Jennings, the two best contestants *Jeopardy!* has ever had on the show.

Since the show, Watson has been used to help treat cancer patients at Memorial Sloan-Kettering Cancer Center. Physicians and analysts at Sloan-Kettering have been programming Watson with clinical data and research from decades of expertise in treating cancer to help them choose the best treatment plans for patients.

The computer system known as Watson competed on *Jeopardy!* against former winners in 2011 and then went on to help doctors diagnose and treat cancer.

Let's go back to the grocery store example. What if the grocery store compared shopping trends of its customers with "likes" on Facebook or "tweets" on Twitter to figure out what might be the next big product? In theory, the store could get ahead of a trend.

Here's another potential use of Big Data. What if the store put radio-frequency identification (RFID) chips on the shopper loyalty card and on the store's shelves to monitor the path the customer takes inside the store. The store could then potentially use this data to improve its sales because it could make changes to that path by changing where products are displayed.

# Chapter 2

# Big Data Equals Big Dollars

Companies have for a long time used data to make business decisions. If a company has a website, for example, it likely tracks how many people visit the site and what they read or watch while they are there. Big and small companies use sales information to make business decisions. If a product is selling quickly, the company will likely stock more of it. Now with Big Data, companies can find much more information about customers. They also can cross-reference their data with other sets of data, such as Internet searches, Facebook and Twitter interactions, and cell phone data, to improve future sales.

Read on for some examples of how Big Data is being used today by companies.

## New Products

Some companies are using Big Data to come up with new products. Netflix, a company that offers Internet streaming of television shows and movies, used data about its customers to come up with original shows.

Netflix, a company that offers Internet streaming of television shows and movies, has used Big Data to come up with new shows.

Netflix has more than thirty million customers. The company collects data about the type of shows people watch, how often they watch Netflix, and what time of day they watch. It can also see how many people finish watching the shows they start, where those people live, what device they use to watch shows, and other shows people scrolled through before picking the programs they wanted to watch. It can even track the volume levels that are used for certain programs, when a show is paused, and when people stop watching a show.

Netflix uses this data—which works out to be hundreds of millions of events—to come up with trends about its viewers. If enough people pause a show or rewind at the same spot, researchers can then zero in on that spot and try to figure out why. The goal for Netflix is to keep people from canceling their Netflix subscription, get new subscribers, and create original programming its audience will want to watch.

Consider the Netflix original series *Orange Is the New Black*, a show about a woman who is sent to jail for a crime she committed a decade earlier. The first week the series became available in 2013, it was viewed more than two previous Netflix-only shows, *House of Cards* and *Arrested Development*. How did Netflix get people to watch the new show? The company used Big Data.

Researchers used data about viewers to figure out that a high percentage of Netflix users liked dark comedies (comedies with disturbing storylines) and stories about prison and crime. They also determined that viewers like it when a female is the lead character. They combined those factors to create *Orange Is the New Black*. Netflix also learned through the data that about 75 percent of its views come from the recommendation section on its homepage. The homepage contains personalized recommendations based on what users have already watched. The show *Orange Is the New Black* was listed among recommendations, and viewers selected it to watch. Netflix didn't have to do a big and expensive advertising campaign to introduce the show, which saved the company money.

## Real-Time Information

Procter & Gamble (P&G) is also using Big Data to make business decisions. P&G has made data about how its products are selling available to thousands of its employees. The company has also set up meeting rooms with large screens displaying data. Managers can then meet in those rooms and use the data to help them make decisions about P&G products, which include everything from pet food to cleaning products to beauty products.

The data shows how P&G products are selling in real time. For example if a product stops selling in a certain area of the world, P&G officials can use the data to determine why and how to fix it. Maybe it had something to do with how the product was advertised or how it was displayed in stores. The information also helps the company come up with new products.

## Predicting Trends

The retailer Walmart is using social, mobile, and retail data to change the way it does business. Walmart created WalmartLabs, a research division, to analyze data about Walmart customers, with the goal of predicting future

The retailer Walmart uses Big Data to figure out what should be displayed in its stores.

buying habits of its customers. For example, by paying attention to what people are saying on social media, such as Facebook and Twitter, Walmart can figure out when talk about college football is starting. Then the company can stock college football products in stores in that area in a timely way, which could result in higher sales.

Walmart and other retailers are also combining economic data with demographic and weather data to figure out what should be displayed in stores and when those items should go on sale.

## Sports

The National Football League (NFL) uses Big Data to set its schedule. The NFL's thirty-two teams play sixteen games during seventeen weeks at different stadiums across the country. To set the schedule, the NFL has to figure out the best matchups, which stadiums are available, which games will be televised, the number of days off for teams, and how far teams have to travel, among other factors. In the past, the NFL figured this out by hand. To get the best schedule, researchers had to sort through seven thousand game options and account for twenty thousand variables and fifty thousand constraints, such as a fair number of days off between games. But now, the NFL uses computer software to come up with the best TV matchups. The goal is to get high television ratings and engage fans.

## Saving Money

Trucking companies are using Big Data to better organize their trucking routes. For example, if a company has one truck, it's easy to set a route from a pickup location to a delivery location. But when there are hundreds of trucks or even thousands of trucks, it can be difficult to organize the fastest and most efficient routes for each driver. Companies use GPS fleet tracking systems to collect data about delivery time, speed, and fuel usage to determine the fastest route, the shortest route, or the route that uses the least amount of fuel.

Trucking and rail companies are using data to organize their routes and keep track of failing equipment.

Companies like Union Pacific Railroad also use data about their engines to watch for equipment that might be at risk of failing.

## Making Money

Video game developers are using Big Data to improve their games by using data about how people play the games. Their goal is to get players to spend more time using the games, increase their in-game purchases, and buy future games.

File   Edit   View   Favorites   Tools   Help

BIG DATA AND JOBS

## Big Data and Jobs

Companies that want to take advantage of Big Data have to hire people who have the skills to turn the data into useful information. They need data-base people to put the data into forms that can be analyzed. They need statisticians who can understand the data. They need managers who are able to understand Big Data and use that information to make decisions. Studies predict that there will be demand for 4.4 million Big Data jobs worldwide by 2015. According to the U.S. Department of Labor's *Occupational Outlook Handbook*, employment for computer and information systems managers is projected to grow 18 percent from 2010 to 2020. Job prospects also look good for statisticians.

Other companies, such as Amazon.com, use Big Data to suggest additional purchases and ultimately sell products. How does this work? A person buys a product on Amazon.com and then immediately sees suggestions for similar products that he or she might like. That list of similar products comes from Big Data.

Many Facebook users have noted their favorite movies, food, and songs as part of their Facebook profile. They type in updates about where they would like to vacation and the type of gifts they would like for their birthday. Facebook can then use that data to target advertising so that when users sign on to Facebook, they will see ads for products they may be interested in purchasing.

# MYTHS&FACTS

**MYTH** Big Data is new.

**FACT** Big Data has been around for a long time. What's new is the computer power available to make sense of that data.

**MYTH** Bigger data is better.

**FACT** Super big databases can be a mess and hard to manage.

**MYTH** Big Data is revolutionary.

**FACT** It doesn't usually take a lot of data to recognize something that is revolutionary. But Big Data helps piece together smaller trends about how to sell a product, analyze sports scores, or fight disease. Someday those small trends might help a lot of people, but in the short term it may not be revolutionary for an individual person.

# Chapter 3

# Big Data Helping the Public

ompanies aren't the only organizations using Big Data to improve their services for their customers. Governments are using it to better serve residents in a more organized way. Cities are using Big Data to better plan public transportation. This includes producing real-time schedules for bus riders in cities such as New York and Portland, Oregon, by using software that tracks the locations of buses. In Philadelphia, Pennsylvania, the city is

Governments are using Big Data to better serve their citizens. For example, Big Data helps officials produce real-time schedules for bus riders in places such as New York City.

using text messaging to survey riders about adding a new transit line to downtown. In Dubuque, Iowa, the city partnered with IBM to create Smarter Sustainable Dubuque. Part of the initiative involved using a mobile app to collect information on how, where, and when volunteer participants travel in the community. The result will improve transportation routes.

Dubuque also completed a water pilot study that involved installing smart meters into Dubuque homes so that citizens can view their home's water usage data and identify leaks. The data, which is updated every fifteen minutes, has led to a decrease in city water usage and an increase in leak detection, according to the city of Dubuque.

## Catching Criminals

Big Data tools are allowing police to find patterns, identify trends, create timelines, and mark maps—all with the goal of catching criminals.

In June 2011, police patrolling Arlington National Cemetery in Virginia stopped a suspicious person. The man turned out to be a sniper who had gone on a spree of overnight shootings more than six months earlier at the Pentagon, the Marines Corps Museum, and Marine Corps and Coast Guard recruiting stations. The police found him because they used data to analyze the previous shootings. The data indicated to police that the criminal was likely to be in a place of military significance, where he could target a rifle over long distances, and close to a major highway. Police began patrolling Arlington National Cemetery and eventually the suspect showed up.

In California, the Santa Cruz Police Department reported a 27 percent reduction in burglaries and a 19 percent reduction in property theft in the year after the department started using Big Data to predict where crimes were likely to take place.

## Traffic

Before jumping in the car to drive across town, some people use Google Maps to see how traffic is flowing. Google gets traffic information from

The city of Dublin, Ireland, is using Big Data to help control traffic congestion.

smartphones. Cell phone companies track smartphone locations. When people pull up a Google map on their phones to get directions, they may also be sending Google data about traffic patterns.

Governments can use this type of data to get even more information about their cities. The city of Dublin in Ireland, for example, is working with IBM to use Big Data to identify and solve causes of traffic congestion. It is using data from many sources, including bus timetables, traffic detectors, closed-circuit television cameras, and GPS updates from the city's buses. Traffic controllers can see the current status of the bus network at a glance and see where delays are happening. This allows traffic controllers to reroute traffic to help keep delays from getting worse.

IBM researchers are working with the city of Lyon, France, to reduce traffic congestion. The system uses real-time traffic reports to detect and predict backups. If an operator sees that a traffic jam is going to happen, the operator can adjust traffic signals to change the flow of traffic. Over time, the system will learn from changes it made in the past that worked and use that information when making future predictions.

## Parking

An app called SpotHero uses Big Data to tell users which parking spots in Washington, D.C., New York, Chicago, Baltimore, Boston, Milwaukee, and Newark, New Jersey, are available. Users types in an address or neighborhood, and they are given a list of available parking garages and lots. The app uses real-time data so that users know which spots are open when they are looking. The driver then selects the parking spot and pays online, and a spot is saved at that garage or lot. If all the spots allotted for SpotHero are reserved, then the garage won't be listed when customers search for parking.

## Politics

Statistician and blogger Nate Silver used Big Data to accurately predict President Barack Obama's win in the 2012 presidential elections against former Massachusetts governor Mitt Romney. Traditional polling suggested that the race would be close. Silver predicted the correct outcome by state by comparing hundreds of poll results, economic variables, demographics, and party registration figures, and by looking at how accurate they were in the past.

## Health Care

Data has been a part of health care for years. For example, hospitals keep information about patients—where they live, their age, the reason they are in the hospital, and other information. They keep track of the average amount of time patients spend in the hospital and the average amount of time they spend in emergency rooms. Health care researchers track the costs of medical procedures, results of

Statistician Nate Silver correctly predicted the presidential winner in all fifty states, and predicted the winner in almost all the U.S. Senate races in 2012.

tests for new drugs, and new medical procedures. With Big Data, all of this information can be looked at together to improve health care.

What if all of this data could tell health care providers who might ask for medical problems before the problems develop? A health care system in Texas called Texas Health is using information from patient records and insurance claims to figure out how to offer high-risk patients help before problems occur.

## Big Data and Rats

You might not think of using Big Data to fight rats, but that's exactly what Chicago is doing. Chicago's non-emergency line, 311, gets about four million calls a year, including from people asking for help controlling rats. Using that data along with data from Carnegie Mellon University, researchers are predicting where and when rat populations will be high. That allows them to stop the problem before it starts.

Another way Big Data is being used in health care is to improve the quality of care. Health care providers can use data as a tool when deciding which treatments to propose. Researchers can use Big Data to determine the best foods to eat and the best exercise routines to follow.

Big Data is also helping reduce the costs of health care. Data can be used to determine which doctors are ordering unnecessary procedures. In the United Kingdom, the National Health Service (NHS) is using data on new drugs to negotiate drug prices.

The National Institutes of Health (NIH) announced in 2013 that it was creating Big Data centers to help the health care community better use Big Data to improve the health care system in the United States.

## Tracking Trends

People use Google to look up information they don't understand or get more information about a topic. Some Big Data researchers are taking the keywords entered by millions of people all over the world to predict trends.

Big Data is being used to predict trends, such as flu outbreaks. This helps doctors and hospitals prepare for sick patients.

Google Flu Trends does this to predict flu outbreaks. When it's flu season, people are more likely to search for flu information. Google has found a close relationship between how many people search flu-related topics and how many people have flu symptoms. That information can be used to figure out how much flu is circulating in different regions around the world. Google Flu Trends provides daily estimates of the number of flu cases, which helps hospitals prepare for patients and notifies residents of a nearby outbreak.

The same way Google Flu Trends predicts flu outbreaks, Adam Sadilek has created a way to track which restaurants may be giving people food poisoning. His system is called nEmesis, and it tracks tweets on Twitter about food. The system looks for when a person tweets from a New York City restaurant and then monitors that Twitter account over the next few days for words like "throw up" or "my tummy hurts." The system assigns a health score based on the tweets, which ends up closely matching the official score from New York's food inspectors.

## Fighting Disease

A company in Cleveland called Explorys is using Big Data to change the health care field. The company uses a Google-like search engine that allows doctors and researchers to search anonymous patient records millions at a time to come up with disease patterns and better treatment options. This allows doctors to figure out the best medication and treatments based on the results of previous patients.

Researchers at the State University of New York at Buffalo are analyzing large databases to look for genetic, clinical, and environmental factors that might help reveal the causes of multiple sclerosis. What they learn might help researchers develop new drugs or help patients manage the disease. Multiple sclerosis is a disease that attacks the central nervous system, which is made up of the brain, spinal cord, and optic nerves. Symptoms may be mild, such as numbness in the limbs, or severe, such as paralysis or loss of vision. The researchers use medical records, lab results, MRI scans, patient surveys, and other sources. They are considering patients' gender, geography, ethnicity, diet, exercise, sun exposure, and living and working conditions.

# Chapter 4

# Big Data and Privacy

When customers buy something at the retail store Target, the product is linked to an identification number for that customer based on his or her credit card, name, or e-mail address.

In an effort to send coupons for baby products to pregnant customers, researchers from Target used identification numbers to figure out which customers might be expecting a baby. An employee told the *New York Times* that the goal was to reach future parents before other stores that sell baby products do. The researchers came up with a pregnancy prediction score, in which they figured out that customers purchased certain products together. Those products were things like a large purse that could double as a diaper bag and vitamins that doctors suggest pregnant women take.

But what if those coupons arrived before the customer told anyone else she was pregnant? That happened in Minneapolis, when a teenager began receiving coupons for baby clothes and cribs in the mail and her father complained to the store. The father found out later that his daughter was pregnant.

Companies like Target have a lot of information about customers, such as the type of cereal they eat and what they like to read. They can use this information to sell products.

Target changed the way it sends coupons when the company realized such coupon targeting was making its customers feel uncomfortable. Instead, the company began sending coupon books filled with a variety of coupons so that customers wouldn't realize they were being targeted.

Companies like Target have a lot of information about customers, including their age, where they live, their ethnicity, their job history, the type of cereal they eat, and what they like to read. The goal for these companies is to sell their products. But for consumers, the question becomes how much information is too much and when does collecting this information violate a person's privacy?

Legally most companies can collect, sell, or share data they have on their customers as long as they tell the customer how they are using the data. But the majority of data scientists who attended a conference in Montreal believe people should worry about privacy issues and the personal information collected about them. Four of five people the researchers surveyed said there should be ethical guidelines for collecting and using data.

Some businesses have guidelines in place. In health care and the pharmaceutical industry, for example, there are guidelines around data obtained from people participating in tests for new drugs or medical procedures.

But guidelines aren't always clear when it comes to companies using Big Data to sell products, especially when it involves social networking. For example, can Facebook and Twitter reproduce information posted by people on their sites without asking permission? And who owns the information—the people posting the updates or the companies? Facebook has been criticized for how it uses information, such as names and images of its nearly 1.2 billion users, to endorse products in advertisements without their permission. The answer to those questions continues to be debated as Big Data becomes more widespread.

## Is Big Data Accurate?

As discussed in chapter 3, police departments are using Big Data to catch criminals. Police use data to predict a criminal's next target. Police can also use Big Data to figure out the chances of a specific person committing a crime. They do this by creating profiles of criminals.

To illustrate the power of Big Data, software developer Jim Adler, who has testified before Congress and the Federal Trade Commission (FTC) on Big Data and privacy issues, created software that could figure out whether a person had committed a serious crime. He used tens of thousands of criminal records and used details such as gender, eye and skin color, whether the person has tattoos, and the number of traffic tickets and minor offenses each person had. His formula, he said, determined with "reasonable accuracy"

Police departments are using Big Data to catch criminals and to figure out a criminal's next target.

whether a person had committed a serious crime. A similar process, he said, could be used to figure out the likelihood of someone committing a serious crime in the future.

Imagine if Big Data showed that a person was likely to commit a crime in the future even though the person had no intention of ever doing anything against the law. Would it be right for people to be questioned based solely on how they looked or where they lived?

The New York Police Department came under fire for the practice of stopping people on the street and searching them for weapons. The majority of people stopped were African American or Latino and were law-abiding citizens who were innocent of any crime. U.S. District Judge Shira Scheindlin found that the New York Police Department violated the constitutional rights of minority residents by making these stops. The judge said police unlawfully subjected black and Hispanic citizens to stop-and-frisk practices based on their race. Lawyers for the city initially argued that the stops matched crime statistics and ultimately reduced crime rates, but in 2014, they announced they would seek to settle the case out of court.

File    Edit    View    Favorites    Tools    Help

THE RIGHT TO PRIVACY

## The Right to Privacy

The National Security Agency (NSA), the United States' top spy agency, collected massive amounts of phone and Internet records from Americans to predict terrorist activity. One of these programs was called PRISM and involved the government collecting data from Internet services like Facebook and Google. The companies and the government have said that the data is collected with court approval and for specific targets, but critics are concerned that the program violates the constitutional rights of U.S. citizens.

## Is It Fair?

Just as Target used Big Data to woo future customers, other companies could use Big Data to decide if a person should be a customer. For example, banks could use Big Data to decide if a customer should be issued a credit card. Using demographic data about the neighborhoods where people live, Big Data could be used to predict whether customers would be able to pay off their credit cards. Health insurance companies could use Big Data to flag people for being at risk of obesity if they have a history of buying plus-sized clothing.

The travel website Orbitz used Big Data to figure out that people who use Mac computers are willing to spend as much as 30 percent more per

When different sets of data are cross-referenced or looked at together, they can provide clues to future trends in everything from business to sports to science to medicine.

night for hotel rooms compared to people who use PCs. Mac users were also 40 percent more likely to book a four- or five-star hotel compared to Windows users, the *Wall Street Journal* reported. So when people searched for hotels using a Mac on Orbitz, they didn't get the best deals. Is that a smart business decision by Orbitz, or is Orbitz using Big Data to unfairly target its customers?

## Is It Worth the Money?

Although there are many examples of how Big Data is being used, it's not clear yet if it's worth the money. Think about the grocery store shopping trip in chapter 1. By using data, the store can track the products sold compared to the weather. The store can see how social media affects sales. It can predict big sellers in the future based on past sales and directly target customers based on what they like to purchase. But will doing all this increase sales?

In the Netflix example, the company is using Big Data to create new shows based on what its audience likes to watch. But data alone doesn't guarantee a successful show. Even if the show has all of the characteristics its audience likes—a female lead character in a story about prison or crime—people won't watch the show unless it is well made. It still has to be a good story that people find interesting to attract viewers. The use of Big Data alone doesn't guarantee success.

Even when a company or organization has a lot of data and researchers to analyze that data, officials still have to figure out which decisions to make based on the data. To do that, they need to understand their customers, patients, or residents and their business the same way they did years ago before all of this information became available.

# GLOSSARY

**analyze** To separate into parts or elements or to examine critically

**Big Data** A collection of data sets so large and complex that it becomes difficult to process using traditional methods.

**blogger** A person who keeps and updates a blog, which is a web log.

**cross reference** A reference made from one place, such as a set of data, book, or index to related material in another set of data, book, or index.

**data** Individual facts, statistics, or items of information.

**database** A comprehensive collection of related data that is organized.

**exabyte** A large unit of computer memory or data storage capacity equal to about one thousand petabytes.

**Google** A search engine people can use to look for information.

**GPS** Global Positioning System; a navigational system involving satellites and computers that can determine the latitude and longitude of a receiver on Earth by computing the time difference for signals from different satellites to reach the receiver.

**petabyte** A large unit of computer memory or data storage capacity equal to about one thousand terabytes.

**PRISM** A government code name for a data collection effort.

**profiling** Using personal characteristics or behavior patterns to make generalizations about a person.

**real-time information** Information that is electronically displayed and up to the minute.

**RFID** Radio frequency identification; a chip that transmits and receives radio waves.

**sabermetrics** Applying statistical analysis to baseball records, especially to evaluate and compare the performance of individual players.

**sensors** A mechanical device sensitive to light, temperature, radiation level, or something similar, that transmits a signal to a measuring or control instrument.

**trend** The general direction in which something is developing or changing.

**unstructured data** Information that is not organized in a predefined manner. Unstructured information is typically text-heavy but may contain data such as dates, numbers, and facts.

# FOR MORE INFORMATION

American Civil Liberties Union (ACLU)
125 Broad Street, 18th Floor
New York, NY 10004
(212) 549-2500
Website: http://www.aclu.org
The ACLU is the United States' guardian of liberty, working daily in courts,
    legislatures, and communities to defend and preserve the individual
    rights and liberties that the Constitution and laws of the United States
    guarantee everyone in this country.

Institute for Data Science
University of Rochester
500 Joseph C. Wilson Boulevard
Rochester, NY 14627
Website: http://www.rochester.edu/rocdata
University of Rochester annual Big Data conferences bring together
    renowned researchers from across the nation, leaders of federal
    research funding agencies, representatives of high-technology com-
    panies, and faculty and students from the University of Rochester for
    presentations, discussions, and networking.

National Freedom of Information Coalition (NFOIC)
Missouri School of Journalism
101E Reynolds Journalism Institute
Columbia, MO 65211
(573) 882-3075
Website: http://www.nfoic.org
The National Freedom of Information Coalition protects the right to open
    government. It is a nonpartisan alliance of citizen-driven nonprofit

freedom of information organizations, academic and First Amendment centers, journalistic societies, and attorneys.

Open Data Foundation (ODaF)
5335 North Nina Drive
Tucson, AZ 85704
(650) 331-7375
Website: http://www.opendatafoundation.org
The Open Data Foundation is a nonprofit organization dedicated to the
    adoption of global standards and the development of open-source
    solutions promoting the use of statistical data.

Pew Internet & American Life Project
1615 L Street NW, Suite 700
Washington, DC 20036
(202) 419-4500
Website: http://www.pewinternet.org
The Pew Internet & American Life Project is one of seven projects that make
    up the Pew Research Center, a nonpartisan, nonprofit "fact tank" that
    provides information on the issues, attitudes, and trends shaping
    America and the world. The project produces reports exploring the
    impact of the Internet on families, communities, work and home, daily
    life, education, health care, and civic and political life.

Research Data Canada
Website: http://rds-sdr.cisti-icist.nrc-cnrc.gc.ca
Research Data Canada is a collaborative effort to address the challenges
    and issues surrounding the access and preservation of data arising from
    Canadian research. This multidisciplinary group of universities,

institutes, libraries, granting agencies, and individual researchers has a shared recognition of the pressing need to deal with Canadian data management issues from a national perspective.

## Websites

Due to the changing nature of Internet links, Rosen Publishing has developed an online list of websites related to the subject of this book. This site is updated regularly. Please use this link to access the list:

http://www.rosenlinks.com/DIL/bigdata

Craig, Terence, and Mary E. Ludloff. *Privacy and Big Data.* Sebastopol, CA: O'Reily Media, 2011.

Cukier, Kenneth, and Viktor Mayer-Schonberger. *Big Data: A Revolution That Will Transform How We Live, Work, and Think.* New York, NY: Houghton Mifflin Harcourt, 2013.

Harris, Nancy. *Mashed Potatoes: Collecting and Reporting Data.* Vero Beach, FL: Rourke Publishing, 2008.

Hurwitz, Judith, Alan Nugent, Fern Halper, and Marcia Kaufman. *Big Data For Dummies.* Hoboken, NJ: Wiley, 2013.

Lewis, Michael. *Moneyball: The Art of Winning an Unfair Game.* New York, NY: W. W. Norton & Company, 2004.

Milton, Michael. *Head First Data Analysis: A Learner's Guide to Big Numbers, Statistics, and Good Decisions.* Sebastopol, CA: O'Reilly Media, 2009.

Rose, Kathryn. *Staying Safe on Facebook: A Guide for Teens.* Seattle, WA: CreateSpace Independent Publishing Platform, 2012.

Swam, Brat. *How Am I Doing ?: A Big Data Approach to Life—Wealth, Health, Family, Children, Education.* Seattle, WA: CreateSpace Independent Publishing Platform, 2013.

Wingard-Nelson, Rebecca. *Data, Graphing, and Statistics Smarts!* (Math Smarts!) Berkeley Heights, NJ: Enslow Publishers, 2011.

# BIBLIOGRAPHY

Albert, Jim. "An Introduction to Sabermetrics." Retrieved September 18, 2013 (http://www-math.bgsu.edu/~albert/papers/saber.html).

Bertolucc, Jeff. "Data Scientists Talk Privacy Worries." *Information Week*. Retrieved October 1, 2013 (http://www.informationweek.com/big-data/news/big-data-analytics/data-scientists-talk-privacy-worries/240161325).

CNBC. "10 Surprising Ways Companies Use Your Private Info." Retrieved October 1, 2013 (http://www.cnbc.com/id/101044969/page/1).

Duhigg, Charles. "How Companies Learn Your Secrets." *New York Times*. Retrieved September 29, 2013 (http://www.nytimes.com/2012/02/19/magazine/shopping-habits.html?pagewanted=1&_r=2&hp&).

Forbes. "Three Ways To Make Big Data Make Money." Retrieved September 17, 2013 (http://www.forbes.com/sites/ciocentral/2012/06/28/three-ways-to-make-big-data-make-money/2).

Hanchett, Doug. "Playing Hardball with Big Data." Retrieved September 19, 2013 (http://www.emc.com/collateral/article/137534-sports-analysis.pdf).

Hardy, Quentin. "At Procter & Gamble, Toothpaste Is Data." Forbes. Retrieved September 29, 2013 (http://www.forbes.com/sites/quentinhardy/2011/08/03/at-procter-gamble-toothpaste-is-data).

Hill, Kashmir. "How Target Figured Out a Teen Girl Was Pregnant Before Her Father Did." *Forbes*. Retrieved September 29, 2013 (http://www.forbes.com/sites/kashmirhill/2012/02/16/how-target-figured-out-a-teen-girl-was-pregnant-before-her-father-did).

Huffington Post. "NSA Spying Controversy Highlights Embrace of Big Data." Retrieved October 5, 2013 (http://www.huffingtonpost.com/2013/06/12/nsa-big-data_n_3423482.html).

Mahapatra, Lisa. "NSA, Google, Facebook: They All Watch You and Profit from Big Data Analytics—How Is It Affecting You? Play the Game." *International Business Times*. Retrieved September 23, 2013 (http://www.ibtimes.com/nsa-google-facebook-they-all-watch-you-profit-big-data-analytics-how-it-affecting-you-play-game).

Mashable.com. "5 Ways Cities Are Using Big Data." Retrieved October 6, 2013 (http://mashable.com/2013/09/25/big-data-cities).

Press, Gil. "A Very Short History of Big Data." *Forbes*. Retrieved September 17, 2013 (http://www.forbes.com/sites/gilpress/2013/05/09/a-very-short-history-of-big-data).

Ramaswamy, Satya. "What the Companies Winning at Big Data Do Differently." Bloomberg.com. Retrieved September 26, 2013 (http://www.bloomberg.com/news/2013-06-25/what-the-companies-winning-at-big-data-do-differently.html).

Salon.com. "Big Data Improves Health Care." Retrieved October 5, 2013 (http://www.salon.com/2013/09/09/big_data_improves_health_care).

Thornton, Sean. "Using Predictive Analytics to Combat Rodents in Chicago." Retrieved October 2, 2013 (http://www.govtech.com/data/Using-Predictive-Analytics-to-Combat-Rodents-in-Chicago.html).

# INDEX

## About the Author

Mindy Mozer is a writer and editor living in Rochester, New York, with her husband and two children. She has also written numerous books on digital technology, including *Social Network-Powered Education Opportunities*.

## Photo Credits

Cover and p. 1 (from left) © iStockphoto.com/chienlee, © iStockphoto.com /loops7, iStockphoto.com/loveguli, © iStockphoto.com/denphumi; p. 5 Monkey Business Images/Shutterstock.com; p. 8 pattyphotoart/Shutterstock .com; p. 10 Michael Zagaris/Getty Images; p. 11 Mike Flippo/Shutterstock .com; p. 13 IBM/AP Images; p. 16 Bloomberg/Getty Images; p. 18 Don Emmert/AFP/Getty Images; p. 20 Cristopher McRae/Shutterstock.com; p. 23 Allison Joyce/Getty Images; p. 25 © iStockphoto.com/MichaelJay; pp. 27, 34 © AP Images; p. 29 Alexander Raths/Shutterstock.com; p. 32 Scott Olson/Getty Images; p.36 Arjuna Kodisinghe/Shutterstock.com; cover (background) and interior page graphics © iStockphoto.com/suprun.

Designer: Nicole Russo; Editor: Bethany Bryan
Photo Researcher: Marty Levick